THE
LONG BODY
THAT CONNECTS US ALL

THE
LONG BODY
THAT CONNECTS US ALL
Poetry

RICH MARCELLO

Langdon Street Press

Langdon Street Press
2301 Lucien Way #415
Maitland, FL 32751
407·339·4217
www.langdonstreetpress.com

Printed in the United States of America

ISBN-13: 9781545611944

Also by Rich Marcello

The Beauty of the Fall
The Big Wide Calm
The Color of Home

Read more about Rich Marcello and his work at:
www.richmarcello.com

IN MEMORY OF MY FATHER
AND DONNA ANCTIL,
BOTH WHO LEFT THIS WORLD MUCH TOO SOON

Contents

Part III – Aether

Part I — In the Coming

A Piece of Bark

I go into the woods behind my house
searching for a tree just my age.
I cut from it a jagged piece of bark
in your memory.

I place the bark between my hands,
scraping back and forth until I see red,
until I see every gurgling, blue-faced,
moment from our helpless night.

I know the tree is in great pain now
as vulnerable as I am,
having lost its armor, its beauty,
its guide, its sleeve of hope.

I will visit this place often,
to watch the tree heal,
to grieve what I have done
and what I have lost.

Existential Bullets

His father was wild.
Or brilliant.
Or broken.
Or silver-tongued.
Or violent.

Take your pick.

One summer night,
the man shot squirrels
from the front porch
with a semi-automatic rifle
as he taught the boy
about Kierkegaard.

After that, he, just a teenager,
too young to know better,
did the only thing he could:

He followed.

I Do Now

When you cast
your lodestar my way,
I basked in love.
I became the hologram king,
the warrior spirit,
the lover of light.

I didn't know then
that a lodestar's intensity
is inextricably linked to its shadow,
and that left unnourished,
it will darken with time.
I didn't know then
how to become more than
a hologram, a spirit or lover,
or how to accept your shadow
as much as your light.

The Erie Lackawanna

On the train ride to my hometown,
I forget all I've learned about
being vulnerable, opening or crying.
His shoes are too big again.
The train is accelerating toward the past,
on the verge of becoming a runaway.
Your smile, generous, no longer widens.

You take my hand anyway,
gently circling your thumb around my palm,
as you speak of working through a place
I thought I'd put behind me more
than a few times.

The past circles, doesn't it?

Your beautiful sleeveless red dress,
the white pearls your grandmother gave you,
your blonde hair pulled back in a ponytail,
the scent of your favorite perfume,
all conjure me back.

The strength on your face is daunting.

We circle until I find my own steady,
until I remember we men, too,
are sometimes passengers on a cattle car,
trying to find our way back to
a place that no longer exists.

Blue Gears

The blue gears took hold and
tried to turn me
like the others
into the sum of parts

The worker of power, of money
The father, the son, the ghost walker
The lover, the projection, the artist

And while those parts come and go like
tall waves, stage personas parading,
heroes or villains warring,
they're not me

I'm a witness sitting in the big chair,
a student of mysteries,
striving to grind down
abundant but finite gear teeth,
not only for me,
but for all those lost in blue

Porchwork

You come home from work
with metal pieces in need of straightening,
the result of an earlier errant production run.
For ten dollars, I spend my Saturday
on the front porch running thousands
of bent rods, of scrapworks,
through a straightening machine

On occasion, I gaze outward
into the woods, aware
that my increasing sense
of accomplishment
mirrors the rise of the sun.
Finally, when it's dusk,
you come to the porch
to see me, your nine-year-old son,
to offer payment, but it's the warmth
on your face that stirs me the most

I know you're proud of me
for sticking with the cogs
and crooked metal.
I know you love me.
I know I've somehow taken
a step toward you

Today, building a Lego set on the floor
with my son, I realize I've been trying
to duplicate that moment on the porch
over thirty years now, my entire work life

No Need for Cowboy Boots

A provocation from the groundless,
a hymn for the spun-out,
when the sirocco winds came,
at first I stood my ground
and professed

separateness

individualism

strength.

That's what we do here
in the dust and dirt.

Slowly though, I couldn't resist.
I lost my footing, lifted off and connected
with the seekers, the mystics,
the riders of the hot and cold drafts,
more abundant than I imagined,
who had surrendered before me
and discovered that plunging
and soaring are equals when
ground is an illusion.

The First Grandson

Shiny quarters given
your workday suits and ties, even on the weekends
the fights on the old radio in the basement
the cherry trees in full bloom
the Jersey shore strawberries
our long talks over football

I was the long-awaited grandson,
endeared by order and substitution,
the son never to come.
A circle in a square
Hair always a little too long
Values a little too left
I often yielded back then
I thought out of respect
but now I know out of descent

You taught me first
that love amidst difference,
like hydrogen on the sun
fusing into helium,
lights generations.

Labor Day Pastoral

Labor Day caps two weeks of vacation
far from the suit-strain and stress of work.
This screen porch becomes a refuge,
the fine metal mesh comforting
in its transparency.

The sun breaks through the trees and skylight,
mottling my Adirondack chair and me
with badges of light, as if I was embedded.

The woodpeckers and chipmunks sound off
from the surrounding forest, a dense fugue
in the making, previously unheard,

the tomatoes and watermelons seem to grow
before me, a ripening blush in our garden plot,

a car races by, its driver
thriving on the elixir of distraction.

The sky, the grass, the dirt
are boundless and infinite
in this backyard of mine.
They fill me like you did as a newborn
when I used to spend my lunch hour
sitting in the corner of your bedroom,
chomping on a homemade sandwich,
watching you stretch up and grasp
for the mobile above your crib.

Who would have thought restoration
was possible five years ago,
when ambition, money, sex,
each numbing in its own way,
eclipsed the deep-seated beauty
of the rhythm of life

Daughters and Sons

Go down now, my love,
deep inside to that place where the unimaginable took hold,
to that place where you broke a thousand times over.

There, kiss the pain. Embrace it as a child until you can release
into a tender broad-minded breeze that carries you far out onto the ocean.

When you can see no land behind you,
when there's nothing in front of you but water and sky,
lift off and soar high above the past.
Stay in the refuge as long as you need, until you
forgive not only those who harmed you, but yourself, until you know you
already have all you need. It was only clouded over for a time.

When you return to shore, may you know that the love you send out
to all those who hate, to all those who suffer, to all those stuck
in judgment, to all the daughters and sons, will one day heal the world.

A Father in the Dark

Sometimes, when I'm dark
like now, you visit,
hands pocketed and
smile worn calm

Without a word,
you remind me of how
you believed in me
before I did, of how
father is a name that
can apply to anyone,
of how a brief blush
of peace, of forgiveness,
can come when
least expected

To Matthew on a Clear Day

Just belong

Say yes to
the lover
the community
the world
yourself

When tempted by
the hum of chaos
or the cage of loss
hold firm
say no and

Just belong

Matchbox

I shovel down for a long time
until I hit ledge. With my bare hands
I search through the dirt
for the *1 Hero* matchbox
I buried as a young man.

Back then,
I locked ten miracles inside,
not knowing one day
I would need them
when this world
I built had
broken me down.

I brush away the remaining dirt,
until I free the matchbox
from the ground.
I slide it open, look inside,
double check to be sure,
and breathe a sigh of relief.

I take out one of the ten
and strike it against
the crosshatched surface.

Tree House

At the cove, up with trees
in the house cantilevered,
we live midair over a lake of dreams
as though we were still
young in our first house.

The smell of the lake below, in heat,
reminds me of the first time
I saw you on the beach.
Blonde hair bleached,
cocoa skin slicked,
your eyes deep,
the dunes stretched behind you in repose.
You smelled like coconut,
like hope realized, like life.
And I thought, well, so this is it.

Let's go down now
to the big oak by the water,
carve the 36th X into its
sturdy and generative bark.

Sunlit and Suffering

His face, sunlit,
reminds me of a time
when I was young,
when I convinced myself
all the world was dark,
when the corner
into which I was painted
seemed drawn by others.

I want to tell him all of this.
Tell him it will be okay.
Tell him he will find his way
out of the corner one step at a time,
even though some will be false.

But I've lived long
enough to know he can't hear me now.
So, instead, I pray forgiveness
washes over him instead
of sunlight.

In the Coming

In sun-soaked morning release the thought-thickets,
the pull-people, the tender weapons, all telling you
to come back, as if returning was a choice, as if another
rubicon hadn't already been crossed.

In translucent fields, step with sure-abandon
and give thanks that you leapt away from
the zealots of continuance.

In the coming, translucence will flesh in with red, blue,
orange, and green, and Kadupul flowers will grow abundant.
Resist the urge to let them wither or the urge to let love
lodge in the past.

In the coming, there will be times of great doubt, of great falls.
Go into them until songs of reflection and release
guide you forward through a lucid lens whose clarity comes
from the mystics and the stuff of crossings.

Part II —Yab Yum

The Blue Line

I went down to the riverbank,
stripped, and waded in up to my knees.
The current, risky, and the other bank,
distant, threatened to turn me around.

I thought of you on the day you crossed
and remembered the stenciled words
on the back of your t-shirt:
To thrive, I accept a thousand deaths.
To thrive, I begin over and over.

The water temperature dropped below
hope, until a blue line divided my upper
and lower legs, until I couldn't shake the cold.
The sky, Cimmerian, sprinted in from the west,
confirming I would never possess your strength.

Downriver,
a large snapping turtle
on the return trip from higher ground
lumbered toward the water,
surrounded by the aura of birth,
until she disappeared below the blue line.

Then I dove in.

Thanksgiving

We had a thankful day, didn't we?
One filled

with family,

    food,

        football,

with touch more generous
than usual.

You had this uncertain look on your face
the last time I saw you in the rearview mirror,
as if you could see around the bend,
as if you were ready and not ready
to say goodbye, but you waved
as we pulled away.

I guess, in the end, none of us knows
what's to come except when we do.

When Blood Thickens

c.

Loss has its own light.
In the throng
you can always
pick out the ones
who've been hurt the most,
the ones who are beacons
toward the kindhearted age.

cc.

If you choose me
if I am your chosen
if our blood thickens
to brother,
to sister,
if others do the same,
then know this:

Together, we will heal.

ccc.

You calmed me
with denial-busting incantations.
You helped me ward off fear and map
out a centered path forward.
You gently convinced me that all
these years of trials were not in vain,
but in preparation for these shaded times.
You reminded me that, now, more
than ever, we must elevate accountability
and responsibility within.

23

The Search for Solid Ground

We swam out in a pack
island-searching in an endless sea.
Family, old lovers.
Mentors, old friends.
You and me.

One by one,
the others turned back,
until we were the only two left
bobbing in the mulish waves,
the sun above us nearing west.

You smiled,
kissed me softly on the cheek,
a tender reminder of why
I'd come that far,
and sent me on my way.

Then you floated, as if you
believed weight was an illusion.

As I swam off, I kept looking
over my shoulder,
watching you peacefully glide along,
until the tiny dot of you merged
with the sunset.

Senior Year English Class

You were standing in front of the class
leading us through some boring topic,
a dry essay overshadowed by your intoxicating
combination of wisdom and grace.
I thought you could coax me out of the granite stone.

A year standing side by side,
turning Shakespeare and Pynchon into vessels of connection
where death plots and conspiracies held little weight
as long as we were talking.

We were always building off the stories,
laughing about the woes of introverted writers,
pushing the edges of honesty, intimacy
that only previously existed for me on the page.
We overturned all the norms
some of them even meant to be broken,
and through touch and words forged a connection
so deep, so generative,
that I was sure Kadupul flowers would rise
and bloom from the granite cracks.

Was the love real or imagined?
At year's start, I was a boy.
I was a cenotaph.

How We Struggle to Pass Down

He speaks, with pauses,
about all that is ahead.
Money. Work. Women. Love. Family.

I want to tell him
to be young again
               with dreams
is much the same
as to be old
               with regrets.

I want to tell him
he already has what he needs,

tell him that we only love
a moment at a time, that his choices will
define him, that love will guide
him through.

Then I remember a young man his age,
convinced he knew better
than the men who came before him.
I remember what I must embody now:
he'll have to learn on his own.

Stillness

There is nothing like the stillness
When it's time for me to heal
A light of rediscovery
A gift
A reprieve

There is only a fan spinning
In the room where I sit
A castle in the air circling endlessly

Every now and then I visit this place
To stop circling
To forgive myself
To let go of ambition arrogance

Here the fog lifts over intimacy
I can see myself
All that I love
I can see the road as home
Contentment as change
I see you

I am learning to accept what comes
Even to embrace us without expectation
I will stumble again
That much seems inevitable
I may lose sight
You may lose sight of me as well
That's why I want you to see me now
Remember.

The Ocean in Spring

Love,

I'm underneath the rules,
the responsibilities,
underneath seven generations
of fathers who taught me
this place is what all men desire.
This gilded armor, unknowingly
built up over the years,
has trapped me.

I want to feel the ocean breeze again,
ride the waves to shore, taste the salt
water, and bury my toes in the sand
as I did as a boy.

I am breathlessly trying to will your arrival.
I want you to labyrinth in
and find me at the core.

I want to walk out of here hand in hand,
unbound over the scorched earth,
past those still caught up,
toward release,
toward emancipation,
toward the land of open
where truly feeling is welcomed,
and an examined life is common.

I'm ready.

Messengers of Hope

I spent a year working on something
I believed in,
a blueprinted intention
I thought would make
a difference

In the end I failed
not for lack of trying
nor for lack of honest work
but for not recognizing
that cursory men
with power create
their own truths

I don't know why I feel
so heavyhearted tonight
Maybe because of those
who came before you
Maybe because,
as we spoke over elbow-handshakes
of what's next, your eyes,
filled with contempt and pleasure,
left me with one less friend

I do know that I will learn
from this in time,
but for now I let pills
stream me to sleep
May I dream of
vibrant wounded healers
carrying tellurian balms
instead of what-ifs

In the rough patch

the fog rolls in,
blinding hope with alabaster
promises, stealing breath.

I struggle here for a time, lost,
tethered to a thin
steel and glass thread,
until I remember
this part, too, is exactly
what I wanted.

To stand
resolute and vulnerable.

To see
both the jagged and the pristine.

To love fully
and feel all of the consequences.

The Sentinels

When sudden
change comes,
as it often will,
resist the urge
to shut down

Your stock gone bust
A cultivated job lost
The death of a father
The leaving of a love
A stealing of faith in yourself

Instead,
each time subsidence looms,
practice opening a fraction wider,
until, after slogging more than any sane
man could fathom, you know
your life is flowing as intended,

and the suddens are only
sentinels of love in disguise.

Cinderworks

The men,
the stoic men.

With their spunout
power,
money,
control,
silence.

With their empires,
small and large, with their
cinderworks and tall walls,
guarding stone dreams.

Somewhere during the slow burn,
I moved away from them,
a sailboat wafting away
from an oil-slicked harbor,
a pilgrim determined to sob again.

The Scout

Up in the trees,
in the lookout and well-defended,
the scout studied the horizon
steadfastly waiting for his arrival.

He stilled and focused, as he was taught.
When his thoughts drifted to gold,
to her, to the city from which he came,
he didn't judge them
or his less than perfect profession.

There were so many ways
for him to lose himself below.
Were there any city dwellers
who hadn't, at least for a time?
But how long could he
hold the horizon?

When he returned to his breath,
he noticed that he'd opened briefly,
an ephemeral witness,
to all that kept him from himself.

The Return of the Hippies

Incense nights and peppermint skies
joined bodies, fingers and sweat
the sweet taste of you on my tongue

Go back to those
flower-bright, earthen days
and touch that magnificent
version of yourself.

Put on the long beads,
grow your strawberry blonde hair
to the middle of your back,
squeeze into bellbottoms
as wide as the sky.

Return to that forgotten place
where life was an experiment,
where love freed us,
where the sun and the silence
conjured hope and rainbow dares.

Remember that surreal time,
where our birthright
was to fill the world,
like John and Yoko,
with songs of possibility.

Then go out into this fractured world.
Love. Be kind. Be generous. Be resolute.
We only have a hundred
years left to turn
the ship we built,
and we need billions
of small acts to
save us.

Fleck

I go down
as far as the deepest idea will take me,
and still it isn't far enough.

Out of the corner of my eye,
I swear I see you, before all the trouble,
your knowing smile still intact,
wearing only my Beatles t-shirt,
dancing to "Come Together" in our living room.

That smile
reminds me of the time we were in Willow Park,
and I was pushing you higher.
Or where you pushing me?
Memory is far less reliable down here.

Further down, out of reach, I see a fleck of light,
a small bud of red mist in a slate sea,
but I can't muster the strength to move closer.
Then, as if grace does exist, all my old thoughts
release and bubble-up toward the surface.

I fall, slow at first,
a buckling down the scree.
When I touch down on the bud,
softer and larger than I thought,
not one, but hundreds of white lotus flowers
bloom all around me.
I smile like you did that day in the park.

White Poppies

Over time,
peace came violently.

In the passing glances of look-a-likes.
In nights of sweat and fear.
In the waves crashing against the cliffs,
changing everything or nothing depending
on my drug.

Each time, amidst the anarchy,
I thanked you for leaving and
for living your life,
so I could live mine.

And then one day,
as I stood in a clearing, dense woods
encroaching from the perimeter,
white poppies bloomed en masse,
affirming my chant of thanks
as transcendent seeds.

Yab Yum

We're facing each other in yab yum position,
your arms on my shoulders,
your forehead barely touching mine.

We stay this way until our breath syncs.
Then we kiss, gently at first, taking our time,
confirming the wisdom of slow builds.
All along the way, I try to keep the worry
about the inevitable from my eyes.

I want you to break in.
Push through to the inside
Sit with me face to face
until I see dance in the great fall
Laughter in the giant sob
Bliss in old pain
Love in loss.

I want to practice Kabbasah on the floor,
as we did at our start, bathing each other
in spinning wheels of light,
balancing movement and non-movement,
your stilling fingers, barely touching lips, and
ample sweat my gentleness guides.

And for a time you give me all of this.
Easing me in. More fully aware.

Then you say:
My love, we all fall apart.
We all pass. We all let go.
You will begin again
a thousand times, and so will I.
You must bronze your cut
so you'll never forget
there is no such thing
as a perfect love.
You must learn to drink
from the fountain of you.
You've been thirsty far too long.

37

Part III —Aether

Timeservers

We men
use a trick.

When descending,
we appear to ascend.

When broken,
we appear indestructible.

And when alone,
we work hard
to not forget
how to simply appear.

Belong to No One

Belong to no one except yourself.

In times of great love, take a deep
breath and remember love is fullest
when you don't lose yourself.

In times of great loss, belong,
but do not linger.
Accept generous caresses, forgive
for things said human, and remember
only the form of connection changes
after death.

On most days, days of normal hours,
fill the small simple moments
with kindness and compassion,
and belong to no one
except yourself.

Whispers and Personas

I read between the lines,
the multi-threaded glances
the whisper-whispers.

I've moiled away
in this place for a long time,
this warren of hole-and-corner
passageways and slate walls,
this place where you've
learned to thrive.

But I'm tired now.

I just want you to say
what you mean once more.

Just tell me what you believe
as you did when you wore
love's first mask.

Black Belt

Go back to when you were a boy
to the place where shame parades
to the room where your father
took out his black belt
told you to toughen up
told you to take it like a man.

Put your arm around your younger self
and tell the boy it will be okay.
Then, as you're walking out together,
light a match to the
gasoline-soaked rag ball
you pieced together for far
too long and toss it behind you.

Under the weeping willow

out of plain view in our secret place,
the light snuck in through
the dense drooping branches,
as we sat on a blue blanket.

You undressed me that day,
pulling off my black t-shirt before yours,
feeding me spoonfuls of the tree's
milky medicine sap,
as we pushed through the past.

Then at the open or close moment,
when I didn't think transcendence was possible,
you showed me how to cry softly,
not from loss, but from the knowledge
that pain, even there, was inescapable, and that
once delivered, it didn't have to linger
or drain joy for long.

After that,
for a time,
life was a little easier.

The Mess in the Rearview Mirror

Embrace the violence in the walls.
The whispers from those who still believe they're immune.
The men who blame you instead of themselves.

On open highways, love autumn spirits
who see the beauty and grace
still in you from before the fall
and who know this world is full of extremes,
one of which you were lost in only for a time.

How to Be a Good Man

When you want to shut down, open.

When you want to lash out,　　　embrace.

When you want to walk away,　　　　　move closer.

When you want to hate,　　　　　　　　love.

And when you can't do any of these things,　　　forgive.

The Walking

Today persistent snow creates
a white ceiling and swirling walls around us
as we walk through the morning.
Mostly we walk in silence, aware
we're connected to some larger
radiant web, to some ageless dance,
ubiquitous on days like today.

A car rumbles by, its young occupants
tangled in words. We speculate they're trying
to understand the push-pull of early love,
of souls newly joined who haven't yet
learned how to walk together and alone.

Our hands join, fingers interlaced.

Later, as we turn onto the wooded path leading home,
we see the same car stopped but running.
We try not to notice as we pass, but can't help but catch
a few images through the lightly-steamed windows.

Light and dark hair intermingled.

Breasts partially sweatered.

A pleated skirt raised.

At home, clothes fall off.
Face to face, we tremble as we kiss,
in a way that can only happen
after years of walking.

Out of the Straits

As a young man,
the peaks, often too high,
and the valleys, often too low,
ruled me.

The blonde hair, blue eyes
The tabs and ounces
The towers of coin
The straits of fame
The brokers of power

Now, I accept all landscapes
The Peaks. The Valleys.
And the cities, meadows,
and forests in between,
often filled with simple things,
where I mostly live.

How to Leave the Modern World

I went into the white room, a deprivation chamber of sorts,
and strapped into the oak chair.
On the table next to me, a razor rested between
an upright bundle of sage and enough water for the long haul.
I lit the bundle and shaved my head, thinking both might help.

For days, nothing came except cold sweats
and warm thoughts of the return.
I had many full rooms outside of that one,
chock full of objects once coveted—
the European cars, the gold bullion, the Kandinsky.
I left behind a love, too, waiting for me
to abandon the white room for good.

When my water had run out, when I had all but
given up, strange symbols, runic I think, each a vibrant color not
of my world, materialized on the walls.
I studied them for what seemed like a long time
only to conclude they were indecipherable.
Then a thick mist, scented orange, clouded and warmed the air,
and from a location I couldn't pinpoint, a woman whose voice
reminded me of my grandmother's, began a hymn.
While I couldn't make out her words,
the melody so moved me that I began to sob.
A door directly in front of me materialized.

I unstrapped myself, pushed off the oak, and went through the door,
only to find another white room, completely empty.
I sat on the floor cross-legged, closed my eyes,
and focused on my breath
until I understood the spectacular beauty and horrific violence I
left behind had somehow skewed in modernity,
until beauty and violence rebalanced,
until the paradoxes our ancestors had known became
my language, until my only thought was, *Oh my.*

Men on the Verge

Today
on this start
of a new year,
we seem on the verge.
Will this be a year of
hope or fear,
right or wrong,
love or hate,
war or peace?

We spend so little time
in uncertainty,
in this shaping place
full of possibility
instead opting for the cloudy illusions
of steel, stone, and glass.

Sometimes I wonder
what the world
would be like
if we spent each day
on the verge,
waiting calmly
for whatever comes.

We who come from loss

trust the fall more than the spring
sunset more than sunrise
the end of love more than the beginning

but one day,
past the numbings
the far off mystics, some wise
the mentors, some false
the endless senseless hurtings
and the hard-earned healings,
past the silence of your father,
the vocations of betrayal,
the way she left you when you grew too afraid,

blue sky will no longer weigh you down
seeds of doubt will cease to bloom
You'll birth your own providence
and become the sunrise and the sunset,
the seasons, and above all else,
resolved

The Big Leap

You're on the opposite bank,
though it could be the opposite
side of the world.

The sun, as ultimate trickster,
highlights your beautiful golden hair,
your serene face, and
widens your smile a bit.

You're thinking about the big leap,
the joy of it, and the fear, too.
You're wondering
if I'll cut through the dark,
still thick on this bank,
and join you midstream.
You're hopeful that I'm ready this time,
that I'll overcome my fear of flow,
and together we'll finally ride downriver.

But here's the thing about the big leap.
Even joined, even in daylight,
neither of us knows what
will happen in the unrelenting, gelid rapids.

Still, here I come, wearing
freshly woven Alpaca cloth,
praying it's not too late

Searchers in a Slowly Lit Room

Deep underneath
where words radiate, radiate
you listen,
on occasion gently guide
like a monastic

I feel connected here
to something larger
pulling at me to go now
and not wait any longer,
as if finding my way through
was a choice

I've dreamt, like my forefathers, of
touching the Himalayan sky
swimming the Sargasso Sea
going deep into the Carlsbad Caverns
climbing the redwoods at Muir

more of
walking next to her and being utterly wild,
helping her go wherever she needs to go,
holding her even when I'm most afraid
praying she will do the same for me

most of
standing resolute in a venerable forest
filled with red oaks
and pine pitch blossoms

In a way, I do the work alone,
you as my witness.
In a way I do the work connected,
you as a fellow searcher,
linked by the old soulful
immeasurable mystery
of the once lost.

Passing

I saw you the other day,
standing in the evergreens with your arm around our son,
your hair short again like when we were young
and an aura around you I hadn't seen in a long time.
Its hue, dense and golden, radiated contentment and
reminded me of how far we've come.

In the days past, you were always spinning hope
on our medicine wheel. As a mother, a daughter,
a career woman, a lover, a wife.
And though I didn't know it then, I was already
here, flung into our future, watching, spinning in my own way,
searching for some way back.

In this place of no recourse you have time to hone truth.
Whittled down, I say now, we spent most of our time
holding on too long or too little.
Rarely did we recognize, never mind accept
the natural coming and going of a life joined.
For if we had, we would have been face to face
with the uncertainty into which we are all born,
and perhaps that would have freed us.

Many would say I learned this too late, that I killed love,
that given infinite chances, I, a chrysalis,
cracked now and then, but never fully emerged.
To them I would say, the story unfolded as intended,
even the most difficult parts.
I would say, none of us can harm love in its
absolute form, the radiant web that connects us all.
No, we only harm the shapes it takes, the ones that were
never meant to be more than passing

Two

On a gentle summer day, under a canopy
of leaves and grapes, we ate and drank
to the mystery of twos.

The sunlight, undeterred,
mottled your holy brown skin
until I was sure you had taken back
your hope and strength,
both entrusted to me for far too long.

You had an aura around that day, filled
with grace, one that restored what you'd lost long ago.
The glow reminded me that there's nothing more
precious than when two passengers, unsure and true,
let love level them.

Doorways

There are doorways,
all of them illusions.

Because once
you're in,
you know
you've always been.

Poems and Prejudice

Over time, I've seen things I hoped
I never would. Sudden violent death.
Shallow men with power creating their own truths.
The loss of innocence. The hardening of love.

Still there are days when the morning light
on Bare Lake takes my breath away, or a new
song from an old master
transports me into the moment.

Poems and prejudice all mixed up, day
after day, year after year. Sometimes
I wish I was your age again, except I don't
want to give up the hard-earned wisdom.
I want to take it back with me thirty years
so I can go further than I made it
this time around. But we don't get do-overs,
do we? Not even through our children.

Young distant stranger,
so gifted, so full of life.
If only for a brief moment,
I want you to see me
clearly in the night.

The Long Body

Let love guide you now into
sun soaked days and bliss soaked nights through
the possibilities in each moment
and in each other.

May each day unfold, deep, wide,
with unwavering kindness, and
if it doesn't, may you each night
forgive love's imperfections.

Remember to lead and follow,
push and pull,
separate and come together,
eyes open to the hooks and distractions
that shave love, some of institution,
some of invention.

When a catch comes, as it often will,
may you meet it with your first kiss and
release it with your last loss,
until you know catches,
even the most difficult ones,
are as intended.

Mostly may you accept the love
in each other and in yourselves.
For it's that gift that lets you see clearly
the long body that connects us all.

Aether

In the trance, I walked down
the winding steps to the water
searching for peace. On the dock,
two rocking chairs waited patiently
like two questions hoping to be answered,
though they might as well have been
a chorus of chairs.

I sat in mine, tapped my finger on its arm
as I rocked, and thought about before.

Off in the distance, proving once and for all
the existence of aether, a man hovered.

And while at first I couldn't make out
his features, when the aether clarified,
I realized there was nothing
in the distance but a reflection, one I'd been
searching for my entire life.

Acknowledgements

Many readers and family have contributed insight and energy to the making of this book. To my wife, Maribeth Marcello, I am deeply indebted. Your regular feedback over the last year on this collection has made all of the difference. You read and worked with these poems more than anyone else, and they are better because of your contributions. I love you.

To my son, Matt Marcello, while this collection is about many things, it's mostly about men, some who are fathers, all who are sons. I hope in some small way that these poems resonate with you as you go forward in your life. I could not be prouder of the man you've become, and it's been one of the great privileges of my life to know you and to watch you grow. I love you.

For their close reading and expert knowledge, huge thanks to Rebecca Givens Rolland, Jennifer Sweeny, Sandra Simmonds, and Michelle Ross Gehan. You are all gifted poets, and I feel blessed and honored to have worked with each of you on this collection.

For helping me remember my love of poetry, I'm grateful to Amy Lynne Johnson. Who knew a few cathartic flash poetry exercises four years ago would lead to a finished manuscript?

For being the first to see the potential in these poems, and for her life-long friendship, I'm thankful to Mary Ellen Fortier. While the world may not be ready for a visual poetry company yet, your unwavering support for my work during the early formation of these poems gave me the much-needed strength to push on and finish them.

Finally, to my dearest friend, Donna Anctil, who passed away in early 2017, I'm thankful for twenty years of generative friendship. One of the highlights of my life was knowing her, walking side by side as a colleague and friend, and seeing her take on the world with love and determination. I bow down one last time.